Fun Fan Facts:
The Unofficial NBA Edition

LA Clippers

Everything Young LA Clippers Fans Should Know

By: Jake Liam

Dedication

To every fan who kept cheering when the scoreboard said otherwise, the seats were half-empty, and the other team in town got all the headlines.

Being a Clippers fan has never been the easy choice. It has been the loyal one. The stubborn one. The one that required actual courage.

This book is for Clippers Nation, past and present. You did not just survive the tough years. You showed up for them.

And to anyone who has ever been the underdog in the room: your era is coming. Ask the Clippers. They built a whole arena to prove it.

THE NBA
BY THE NUMBERS

MOST NBA CHAMPIONSHIPS*

- CELTICS (18)
- LAKERS (17)
- WARRIORS (7)
- BULLS (6)
- SPURS (5)

As of the 2024-25 Season. † One Trophy = 4 Championships.

NBA HISTORY SNAPSHOT

1946 NBA Founded — **1954** Shot Clock Introduced — **1979** 3-Point Line Added — **2023** NBA Cup Introduced

BIG NUMBERS

$156 million
Stephen Curry's est. earnings in the 24-25 season

7'7"
Tallest player in NBA history (Gheorghe Mureşan & Manute Bol)

---

30 Teams Competing in the NBA

4 Playoff Rounds

82 Games Per Season

LA CLIPPERS
IN THE NBA

- FOUNDED: 1970 †
- NBA TITLES: 0
- CONFERENCE TITLES: 0*

56 Seasons in the NBA

*† Founding dates are complicated & may cause arguments at Thanksgiving. Ask someone born before color TV. All Titles reflect pre-relocation franchise history. * As of 2024-25 Season.*

NBA ALL-TIME MVP LEADERS

KAREEM ABDUL-JABBAR (6) ★ MICHAEL JORDAN (5) ★ BILL RUSSELL (5)

EASTERN CONFERENCE

- Atlantic – **Celtics**
- Atlantic – **Nets**
- Atlantic – **Knicks**
- Atlantic – **76ers**
- Atlantic – **Raptors**
- Central – **Bulls**
- Central – **Cavaliers**
- Central – **Pistons**
- Central – **Pacers**
- Central – **Bucks**
- Southeast – **Hawks**
- Southeast – **Hornets**
- Southeast – **Heat**
- Southeast – **Magic**
- Southeast – **Wizards**

WESTERN CONFERENCE

- Pacific – **Lakers**
- Pacific – **Clippers**
- Pacific – **Warriors**
- Pacific – **Suns**
- Pacific – **Kings**
- Northwest – **Nuggets**
- Northwest – **Timberwolves**
- Northwest – **Thunder**
- Northwest – **Trail Blazers**
- Northwest – **Jazz**
- Southwest – **Mavericks**
- Southwest – **Rockets**
- Southwest – **Spurs**
- Southwest – **Pelicans**
- Southwest – **Grizzlies**

Introduction

Welcome, fans! Whether you're new to cheering for the LA Clippers or you've been bleeding the team colors your whole life, this book is packed with fun, exciting facts about your favorite team. Get ready to impress your friends and family with everything you know about the LA Clippers.

Quick Timeout

This book is packed with stats. Like, A LOT of stats. Every fact was checked, double-checked, and triple-checked. But here's the thing about basketball history: not everyone agrees on everything. Ask someone who watched games before color TV and someone who grew up with instant replay and you'll get two completely different answers. My dad, stepdad, uncle, and grandpa all argued about the same fact. Four people. Four answers. All of them think they're right. So if you spot something that doesn't match what you've heard, congratulations. You might be a bigger fan than the people who helped make this book. And honestly? That's pretty cool.

HOW IT WORKS

THE SEASON
82 Games. One Goal.
Each team plays 82 games.
Win enough to make the
Playoffs.
Every game counts!
PLAYOFFS
30 Teams. 16 Make It.
8 per conference make the playoffs.
Win=Advance | Lose=Go Home
Best record
gets home court!
PLAYOFF ROUNDS
Best of 7. Win 4 or Go Home.
4 rounds of pure pressure.
Every series is do-or-die!
OVERTIME?
5 More Minutes.
Keep playing until
someone pulls ahead.
No ties. Ever.
THE FINALS
One Series. One Champion.
Winner lifts the Trophy.
Legend status unlocked.

How the NBA Works

At first glance, basketball feels simple. Ten players. One ball. Two hoops. Go.

Then the NBA adds the layers.

An 82-game regular season. A draft where bad teams pick first. Playoffs that last two full months. Superstars who can change everything with one trade. Dynasties that rise, fall, and rise again.

And somehow, it all works.

The NBA is built on one big idea: every team gets a chance to reset, reload, and rise again. No relegation. No dropping down to a lower league. Just basketball, every night, from October through June.

It is a league designed for drama, stars, and comebacks. And once you understand the flow, it is impossible to stop watching.

The League Setup

The NBA has 30 teams, spread across the United States and Canada. Those teams are split into two conferences:

- Eastern Conference
- Western Conference

Each conference has three divisions, mostly based on geography. Divisions matter for scheduling, but not as much as they used to.

Every team plays 82 regular season games, usually from October through April. Home games. Road games. Back-to-back nights. Long road trips. The season is a marathon before the sprint even starts.

Win games, and you climb the standings. Lose too many, and the pressure builds fast.

How Games Are Played

An NBA game has four quarters, each lasting 12 minutes. That means 48 minutes of game time, plus timeouts, free throws, and the occasional coach argument that adds another 20 minutes nobody planned for.

Scoring is simple:

- A shot inside the three-point line is worth 2 points
- A shot beyond the arc is worth 3 points
- Free throws are worth 1 point

If the score is tied at the end of regulation, the game goes to overtime, which lasts 5 minutes. Still tied? Another overtime. Keep going until someone wins.

There is a shot clock too. Teams have 24 seconds to take a shot. No standing around. No holding the ball forever. Keep it moving.

The Regular Season Race

The regular season is long for a reason. It tests everything.

Depth. Health. Focus. Patience.

Teams play opponents from both conferences, but they face conference rivals more often. By the end of the season, each conference's top teams have earned their playoff spots the hard way.

The goal is simple: make the playoffs. But there is a twist.

The NBA Cup

In 2023, the NBA added something new to the middle of the season. Something with actual stakes. They called it the In-Season Tournament, now known as the NBA Cup.

It works like this: Every team plays a small group stage during November and December, with special court designs that look like nothing else in basketball. The best teams advance to a knockout round held in Las Vegas.

The winners split a prize pool. Players earn bonus money. And for the first time, a team could lift a trophy before the playoffs even started.

Some fans are still warming up to it. Some players love it. But the moment a team starts treating it seriously and a crowd shows up buzzing in December, it feels like something.

Which, honestly, sounds about right.

The Play-In Tournament

Instead of sending the top eight teams from each conference straight to the playoffs, the NBA added something new. The Play-In Tournament.

Here is how it works:

- Teams ranked 1 through 6 in each conference are safe
- Teams ranked 7 through 10 fight for the final two playoff spots

The 7 and 8 seeds have an advantage. Win once and you are in. Lose and you still get one more shot. The 9 and 10 seeds have to win twice in a row just to earn a first-round matchup.

It turns the end of the season into a sprint. Every game suddenly matters more. Fans love it. Coaches age rapidly.

The NBA Playoffs

Once the playoffs begin, everything tightens.

Sixteen teams enter. Eight from each conference. Every round is a best-of-seven games series. That means the first team to win four games moves on:

- First Round
- Conference Semifinals
- Conference Finals
- NBA Finals

Home-court advantage matters. Crowds get louder. Rotations get shorter. Superstars play heavier minutes. One bad quarter can flip a series. One great performance can define a career.

By the time the NBA Finals arrive in June, only two teams are left. One from the East. One from the West. Four wins away from a championship. Four wins away from history.

The NBA Draft: Hope Begins Here

Here is where the NBA gets clever. Every summer, new players enter the league through the NBA Draft. Teams take turns selecting college players, international stars, and teenagers straight out of high school.

The teams that finished with the worst records get the best odds to pick early through the Draft Lottery. It is not guaranteed, but it gives struggling franchises a real shot at changing their future with one pick.

That means one bad season does not doom you forever. It might actually change everything. Some franchises are rebuilt by a single draft night moment.

Hope shows up wearing a new jersey.

No Relegation. All Pressure.

Unlike many global sports leagues, NBA teams never drop down to a lower league. They always stay in the NBA.

That does not mean there is no pressure.

Fans remember losing seasons. Owners make changes. Coaches get replaced. Players get traded. Every year is a test of direction, patience, and belief.

Stars, Systems, and Showtime

The NBA is famous for its stars. But stars do not win alone.

Teams need chemistry. Coaches need systems. Role players need to deliver on the biggest stages. One injury. One hot streak. One trade deadline deal. Any of it can flip a season.

That balance between individual brilliance and team basketball is what makes the league special.

Fast breaks. Buzzer-beaters. Game 7s. And moments that get replayed forever. That is the NBA.

Once you get the flow, it is pure electricity.

LA Clippers Facts

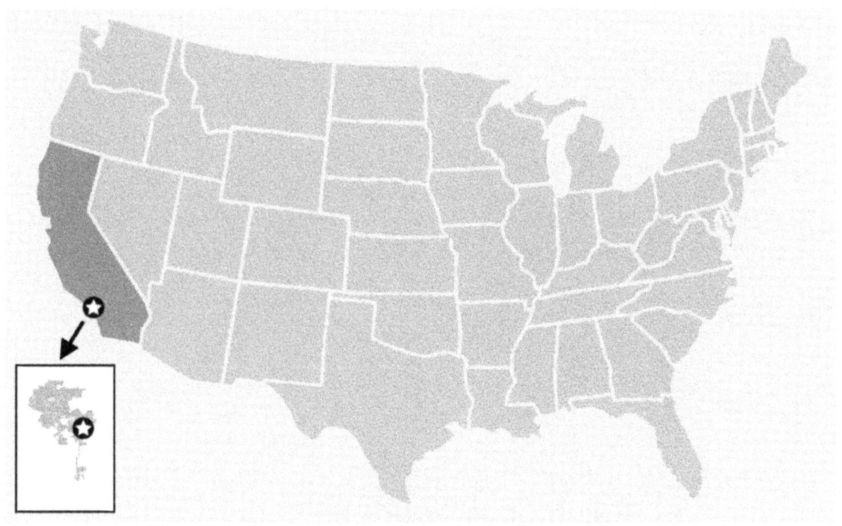

Home City

Los Angeles, California

Metro Area Population

About 13 Million

Home Arena

Intuit Dome

Arena Capacity

18,000

Conference / Division

Western Conference / Pacific Division

Famous Local Food

Korean BBQ, fish tacos, In-N-Out Burger, avocado toast

Chapter 1: From Buffalo to Hollywood

1. Born in Buffalo: The Team That Started Somewhere Cold

If someone told you the LA Clippers were originally from Buffalo, New York, you would probably assume they got the geography wrong. But it is true. In 1970, the NBA handed Buffalo a brand-new expansion team called the Braves, and for a few years, they were actually pretty good. Which makes what happened next even more confusing.

Buffalo sits on the eastern edge of Lake Erie, which means the winters are brutal, the snow is legendary, and the city does not mess around when it comes to chicken wings. The Braves fit right in. They played hard, developed some real talent, and gave Western New York something to cheer about besides the weather forecast. Bob McAdoo, one of the best scorers of the 1970s, wore a Braves uniform and won an MVP award while doing it. More on him in Chapter 2.

The Braves were never superstars, but they were not embarrassing either. They were a respectable mid-tier NBA team in a city that appreciated them. Which is why it stings a little that they were about to get packed up and shipped across the country like a forgotten box of furniture.

2. Westward Bound: San Diego Gets a Basketball Team (Briefly)

In 1978, the Buffalo Braves became the San Diego Clippers, and the name finally made sense. San Diego is a coastal city. Clippers are sailing ships. The ocean is right there. Honestly, it is one of the better team names in NBA history when you think about the geography.

The problem was that everything else about the move was a mess. The team was sold, relocated, and dropped into a market where the NFL's Chargers were already the big attraction. San Diego liked sports just fine, but it wanted winners, and the Clippers were not winners. They had some decent players and a few fun seasons, but mostly they were a franchise figuring out what they wanted to be when they grew up.

Imagine this: you are a kid in San Diego in 1980. The weather is perfect. The beach is fifteen minutes away. You could be doing anything. But you are at a Clippers game, watching your team lose by twenty, and you have to explain to your friends the next day why you went. That was life as an early Clippers fan. Loyal, a little mysterious, and hard to explain at lunch.

The San Diego chapter only lasted six years. By 1984, a new owner had his eyes on a much bigger city.

3. Welcome to LA: Moving Into Someone Else's House

In 1984, owner Donald Sterling moved the Clippers to Los Angeles without much warning and, famously, without the NBA's permission. The league slapped him with a $25 million fine for relocating without approval. Sterling fought it and got it reduced to $6 million. That is a 76% discount on rule-breaking. He paid it and moved anyway. That fine, in hindsight, was the first sign that things were going to be interesting with this particular owner.

Los Angeles already had the Lakers. The Lakers had Magic Johnson. The Lakers were in the middle of one of the greatest runs in NBA history. Moving a struggling franchise into that city was roughly equivalent to opening a lemonade stand next to a five-star restaurant. You could do it. People might even stop by. But everyone knew where they were actually going for dinner.

The Clippers set up shop in the Los Angeles Memorial Sports Arena, which was older, smaller, and significantly less glamorous than the Forum where the Lakers played. For most of the next two decades, the Clippers would share arenas with the Lakers, play second fiddle in their own city, and somehow keep selling tickets to fans who believed, against all available evidence, that things were going to get better.

Some of those fans are still waiting. Others finally got their reward. We will get to that part.

4. The Losing Years: A Decade That Lasted Three Decades

Here is a stat that requires a moment of silence. For nearly forty years, between 1972 and 2011, winning seasons were as rare as snow in Los Angeles. That is not a rebuilding phase. That is a lifestyle choice.

The NBA record for most consecutive losing seasons belongs to the Clippers, who strung together seventeen straight years without finishing above .500 from 1977 to 1993. During that stretch, the league added new teams, retired legends, changed its rules, and invented the three-point line. The Clippers just kept losing. They became so reliably bad that ESPN once called them the worst franchise in professional sports history, which is the kind of honor that comes without a trophy.

What made it especially painful was the draft. The Clippers had high picks almost every year, because bad teams get good picks, and they managed to whiff on most of them. Danny Manning, picked first overall in 1988, was supposed to fix everything. He got injured in his first season and was never quite the same. The Clippers drafted ahead of future Hall of Famers multiple times and still could not find the right combination.

The losing years built something unexpected, though. They built a fanbase that was genuinely different from any other in the league. Anyone still cheering for the Clippers by the mid-2000s was there because they actually loved basketball, not because it was the cool thing to do. That kind of loyalty is hard to manufacture. The Clippers earned theirs the hard way.

5. Donald Sterling: The Owner Everyone Eventually Stopped Defending

Donald Sterling bought the San Diego Clippers in 1981 for just over twelve million dollars. He owned the team for thirty-three years. And for most of that time, he was exactly the kind of owner a franchise cannot afford to have.

Sterling was a real estate billionaire who treated the Clippers more like a tax write-off than a championship contender. He was famously reluctant to spend money on players, facilities, or coaching talent. There are stories, well-documented and extensively reported, of the team traveling on outdated arrangements while other franchises upgraded everything around them. Players who left often had harsh things to say. Coaches rarely lasted long. The organization developed a reputation for dysfunction that followed it everywhere.

Then, in 2014, a recorded conversation became public in which Sterling made deeply racist remarks. The NBA acted quickly. Commissioner Adam Silver banned Sterling for life and forced the sale of the franchise. The Sterling era is an uncomfortable part of Clippers history, but it matters. It explains why the fanbase had to be so patient for so long. It explains why what came next felt less like a transaction and more like a rescue operation. The person who rode in to take over was about to become the loudest owner in the history of professional basketball. You will meet him properly in Chapter 4. He arrives screaming.

6. Bob McAdoo: The Scorer Who Deserved More Credit (1972-1976)

Before the Clippers were the Clippers, when they were still the Buffalo Braves and wearing uniforms that looked like a school project, Bob McAdoo was doing things on a basketball court that most players could only dream about. He won three consecutive NBA scoring titles from 1974 to 1976, averaging over thirty points per game during that stretch, which is the kind of number that makes modern fans do a double-take and ask whether the stats website is broken.

McAdoo was six feet ten with guard skills, which in the 1970s was basically science fiction. He could score from the post, from the mid-range, and from distances that big men simply did not shoot from back then. He won the MVP award in 1975, the same year his Buffalo Braves were one of the more legitimate teams in the Eastern Conference. For a brief, shining window, Bob McAdoo made the franchise that would eventually become the Clippers genuinely must-watch basketball.

The problem is that history has a short memory, and McAdoo spent his peak years in Buffalo, which is not exactly the media capital of the world. He later won two championships with the Lakers as a reserve, which is a deeply ironic footnote for a man who carried a Clippers predecessor on his back. If McAdoo had played those same seasons in New York or Los Angeles, he would be a household name. Instead, he is the answer to a trivia question that most people get wrong. That is worth correcting.

7. World B. Free: The Man, The Myth, The Name (1980-1983)

Lloyd Free legally changed his name to World B. Free in 1981, and honestly, the NBA has never fully recovered from how cool that is. He said it was for the kids, a reminder to be free. Whether you find that inspirational or slightly over the top probably depends on your general outlook on life, but either way, you remember the name. That was rather the point.

World B. Free was a shooting guard who played for the San Diego Clippers in the early 1980s and brought a style of basketball that was part street court, part highlight reel, and entirely entertaining. He was one of the first players to shoot off the dribble consistently from deep range, long before the three-point line became the center of every offensive strategy in the league. Coaches sometimes pulled their hair out watching him. Fans bought tickets specifically to see what he would do next.

He was not the most efficient player in NBA history. His shot selection occasionally made statisticians physically uncomfortable. But Free played basketball like it was supposed to be fun, which in the middle of some truly bleak Clippers seasons was a public service. Imagine This: you are sitting in a half-empty arena in San Diego, the team is down twelve points in the third quarter, and then World B. Free pulls up from thirty feet, looks completely unbothered about it, and drains it. The crowd goes from mildly interested to fully awake in about half a second. That was his superpower, and it was a good one to have.

8. Danny Manning: The Number One Pick Who Never Got His Moment (1988-1994)

The 1988 NBA Draft was supposed to be the day everything changed for the Clippers. They had the first overall pick, and they used it on Danny Manning out of Kansas, a six-foot-ten forward who had just won a national championship and been named the tournament's most outstanding player. Manning was polished, skilled, and widely considered a franchise-altering talent. The Clippers finally had their guy.

He tore his ACL in his first NBA season. Then he tore the other one a few years later. By the time Manning had recovered enough to play consistently, the window that was supposed to define his career had already started closing. He went on to play fourteen seasons in the NBA across multiple teams, made an All-Star game, and had a solid professional career. But the version of Danny Manning that Clippers fans were promised in 1988 never fully arrived, and that gap between expectation and reality became one of the defining images of the franchise's difficult years.

Manning later became a head coach at Wake Forest and Tulsa, which suggests the basketball knowledge was always there, just delivered at a different stage of life than originally planned. The Clippers retired his number 45, which is the organization acknowledging what might have been as much as what actually was. Sometimes a team's history is written in the injuries that changed everything, and for the Clippers, Manning's knees belong in that chapter whether anyone wants to admit it or not.

9. Chris Paul: The Point God Arrives (2011-2017)

When the Clippers traded for Chris Paul in December 2011, something shifted. Not just in the standings, though those changed too. Something shifted in how the rest of the NBA talked about the franchise. For the first time in a very long time, people were discussing the Clippers not as a punchline but as a genuine contender, and the reason had eleven assists, four steals, and an expression on his face that suggested he had already seen every play three seconds before it happened.

Paul was, and many still argue remains, the most complete point guard the NBA has ever produced. His handle was ridiculous. His court vision bordered on unfair. His competitiveness was the kind that made teammates better and opponents genuinely annoyed. He ran the pick-and-roll with Blake Griffin like they had been running it together since childhood, and the combination was so fun to watch that the Clippers suddenly had a national television audience that was not just tuning in for the opposing team.

The stretch from 2011 to 2017, when Paul finally left for Houston, was the closest the Clippers had come in their entire existence to being a true championship-caliber team. They never quite got there, which still stings if you ask the right fans the right question on the right day. But what Paul gave that franchise was something harder to quantify than a title. He gave them credibility. He made being a Clippers fan feel like a reasonable life decision for the first time in a generation. That is not a small thing.

10. Blake Griffin: The Dunk Heard Around the League (2009-2018)

Blake Griffin arrived in Los Angeles as the first overall pick of the 2009 draft, missed his entire rookie season with a knee injury (the Clippers and knee injuries having an established long-term relationship at this point), and then came back in 2010 and promptly won the NBA Slam Dunk Contest by jumping over a car. Not around it. Over it. The hood of a full-sized Kia, with a choir singing in the background, which is either the greatest piece of theater in dunk contest history or the second greatest, depending on your feelings about Jordan's free-throw line effort from 1988.

Griffin was the kind of player who made casual fans stop scrolling. He was a power forward who moved like a guard, dunked like the rim had personally offended him, and developed a mid-range jumper over the years that turned him from a highlight machine into a genuine two-way threat. He made six All-Star teams as a Clipper and became, alongside Chris Paul, the face of the Lob City era that finally gave the franchise a nickname everyone actually wanted to claim.

He was traded to Detroit in 2018, which ended a chapter that Clippers fans are still processing in different ways. Some were angry. Some understood the basketball logic. All of them remember exactly where they were the first time they watched Griffin catch a lob from Paul, rise above a helpless defender, and bring the building to its feet in a way that arena had not experienced in roughly forty years of trying. That is the thing about a great player on a historically struggling team. The moments hit different.

Blake Griffin pushes the ball up the court for the Los Angeles Clippers. Strength. Speed. For years Griffin powered the Clippers with explosive scoring and highlight plays, helping launch the team's exciting "Lob City" era in the early 2010s. *Photo: Blake Griffin. Photograph by Keith Allison. Licensed under CC BY-SA 2.0. Source: Wikimedia Commons.*

Chapter 3: The Moments That Defined a Franchise

11. Lob City: When the Clippers Were Must-Watch Basketball

Around 2011, someone on the internet started calling the Clippers "Lob City," and it spread so fast that even the players started using it, which almost never happens with nicknames invented by strangers online. It fit perfectly because the Clippers, suddenly loaded with athletes who could throw and catch alley-oops at a frequency that felt medically irresponsible, had become the most entertaining team in the Western Conference. This was not a sentence anyone had ever typed before in the history of the English language.

The core of Lob City was Chris Paul throwing, Blake Griffin catching, and DeAndre Jordan doing things near the basket that defied both gravity and the defending player's dignity. Paul had the vision to find Griffin before Griffin had even decided to cut. Griffin had the explosion to get there before the defense had time to panic. Jordan had the wingspan of a small aircraft and the vertical leap of someone who had made a very specific deal with the universe. Put them together and you got highlight after highlight after highlight, served fresh every other possession.

Lob City lasted about six years before injuries, trades, and the general chaos of NBA roster management broke it apart. But during its peak, the Clippers sold out arenas on the road, trended nationally after every other game, and made an entire generation of kids want to learn how to throw a lob pass. That is a legacy. Not a championship, sure. But an actual, genuine, people-still-talk-about-it legacy, and for a franchise that spent decades being discussed mostly in whispers of pity, that counts for a lot.

12. The 2021 Western Conference Finals: The Most Clippers Thing That Ever Happened

Kawhi Leonard, the team's best player and the whole reason the franchise had championship expectations in the first place, went down with a knee injury in the second round against the Utah Jazz. The Clippers were down 0-2 in that series, which meant they needed to win four of the next five games, and the last two without their best player, against a team that had the best record in the league.

They did it. Terance Mann erupted for 39 points in the clincher.

Then came the Phoenix Suns in the Western Conference Finals. The Suns won the first two games. The Clippers fought back with a Game 3 win, but Phoenix pushed the series to 3-1. The Clippers kept battling, winning Game 5 at home to cut the series to 3-2 and keep hope alive. Then the Suns closed it out in Game 6. Kawhi never came back that postseason. It was heartbreaking in the specific way that only sports can be heartbreaking, where you know it is not real life but it still absolutely ruins your Tuesday evening.

13. Steve Ballmer Takes Over: The Loudest Owner in NBA History

When the Clippers went up for sale in 2014, several groups submitted bids. Steve Ballmer, the former CEO of Microsoft and one of the wealthiest people on the planet, submitted the one that ended the conversation. Two billion dollars. The previous record for an NBA franchise sale was around five hundred million. Ballmer paid four times that without appearing to lose a single night of sleep, and Clippers fans who had spent decades watching their owner pinch pennies took that number extremely personally, in the absolute best possible way.

What nobody fully anticipated was what Ballmer would be like as an owner in public. The man is enthusiastic in a way that cannot be faked and probably cannot be medicated away. He shows up to games in full team gear, screaming, jumping, high-fiving complete strangers, and generally behaving like a twelve-year-old who won a contest to sit courtside rather than a billionaire who literally owns the building. Imagine This: you are a professional basketball player trying to focus on a free throw in a crucial moment, and you glance up to see the owner of your franchise, worth roughly eighty billion dollars, doing a full-body celebration in the front row because your teammate hit a mid-range jumper in the second quarter of a regular season game in November. That is Steve Ballmer. Every game. All season. No exceptions.

His arrival changed the culture of the franchise faster than any single trade or draft pick could have managed. He invested in facilities, upgraded travel arrangements, and made it publicly clear that he intended to win. He also announced plans to build the Clippers their own arena from scratch, which after forty years of sharing spaces with the Lakers was the organizational equivalent of finally getting your own bedroom after sleeping on the couch since 1984. The building he built is waiting for you in Chapter 5.

14. DeAndre Jordan's Dunk That Broke the Internet

On January 26, 2015, DeAndre Jordan caught a lob from Chris Paul, jumped over Brandon Knight of the Milwaukee Bucks, and dunked the basketball so hard that the entire internet temporarily lost the ability to think about anything else. Knight ended up on the floor. Jordan stood over him for a moment that the cameras caught and the internet preserved forever. It became one of the most shared sports moments of that decade, spawned about four hundred memes before lunchtime, and remains the single image most people picture when they hear the name DeAndre Jordan.

Jordan was the center of the Lob City era and one of the most unique players in NBA history in the sense that he was simultaneously one of the best and one of the most limited players in the league, sometimes within the same possession. He led the NBA in rebounding four times, was a nightmare to score over near the rim, and set screens that opposing players described using words that cannot be printed in a book aimed at kids. He was a force of nature on the defensive end and a genuine weapon in the pick-and-roll game that the Clippers ran better than almost anyone.

He also shot thirty percent from the free-throw line, which is so bad it almost loops back around to being impressive. Teams figured out they could intentionally foul Jordan late in games to stop the Clippers from scoring, a strategy so effective it has its own name, the Hack-a-Jordan, and it genuinely changed how the Clippers could use him in crucial moments. He was the most un-guardable and most foul-able player on the court at the same time, which is an achievement of contradictions that honestly deserves more recognition than it gets.

15. Kawhi Leonard: The Quiet Superstar Who Made Clippers Fans Dream Big

Kawhi Leonard does not do interviews the way other players do interviews. He does not have a loud public personality. He does not post constantly on social media. He famously laughed at an awards show once and it became a viral moment because no one was entirely sure they had seen it before. He is, by modern NBA standards, a complete mystery wrapped in a very large set of hands, and those hands happen to be attached to one of the five best basketball players on the planet.

When Leonard chose the Clippers over the Lakers in the summer of 2019, turning down the chance to play alongside LeBron James to instead help build something in the other half of Los Angeles, the basketball world genuinely did not know what to do with that information. He brought Paul George with him, which made the Clippers the most talked-about team of the entire offseason and briefly convinced the rest of the NBA that the dynasty was finally shifting across town. The Lakers fans were not thrilled. The Clippers fans were not used to winning offseasons and handled it with a mixture of joy and mild suspicion, like someone who finds a twenty-dollar bill in an old jacket and spends ten minutes waiting for the catch.

Leonard has dealt with significant knee issues throughout his time in LA, which has limited how many games he has actually played and kept the championship that seemed so close in 2019 frustratingly out of reach. But when he has been healthy and locked in, he has shown exactly why the Clippers made the bet they made. There is no more complete two-way player in the modern game when Leonard is fully operational. The question of whether he and the Clippers can stay healthy at the same time long enough to find out what they are truly capable of remains one of the most interesting ongoing storylines in the NBA.

Chapter 4: Clippers Culture, Traditions, and Wild Facts

16. Chuck the Condor: The Mascot Nobody Asked For and Everyone Eventually Accepted

The Los Angeles Clippers did not have an official mascot for most of their existence, which is either a sign of dignity or an oversight depending on how you feel about giant costumed animals dancing near the scorer's table. Then in 2016, they introduced Chuck the Condor, a six-foot California condor in a Clippers uniform, and the sports world had approximately forty-eight hours of strong opinions about it before mostly moving on.

Chuck is named after Chuck Person, a former NBA player whose nickname was "The Rifleman," which has nothing to do with condors but everything to do with the Clippers' general approach to branding decisions. He has a beak, wings, red and blue feathers, and the kind of energy that suggests he consumed four energy drinks before tip-off and has no intention of sitting down. He runs onto the court, interacts with fans, fires up the crowd, and occasionally gets involved in promotional activities that make adults laugh and kids absolutely lose their minds, which is exactly what a mascot is supposed to do.

The California condor was an inspired choice when you think about it for more than twelve seconds. The condor is one of the largest flying birds in North America, nearly went extinct, spent years being carefully protected and slowly brought back, and is now thriving again. If you wanted a mascot that accidentally doubles as a perfect metaphor for the Clippers franchise, you could not have done better if you tried. Chuck the Condor is, without meaning to be, deeply poetic. He is also extremely goofy looking, which the Clippers have fully leaned into. Good for them.

17. Forty Years of Somebody Else's Building

For four full decades, the Los Angeles Clippers paid rent to share an arena with the Los Angeles Lakers. Let that settle for a moment. The Clippers moved to LA in 1984, and from that day until 2024, they played their home games in a building that also hosted their most famous rivals, had the Lakers' championship banners hanging from the rafters, and was generally considered Lakers territory by anyone who walked through the doors. It was the longest, most expensive, most psychologically complicated roommate situation in the history of professional sports.

First it was the Los Angeles Memorial Sports Arena, which they shared briefly. Then it was the Great Western Forum, the Lakers' legendary home. Then it was Staples Center from 1999 onward, which was rebranded as Crypto.com Arena in 2021. The Clippers paid to play there just like the Lakers did, but every banner above them belonged to someone else, every retired jersey on the wall belonged to someone else, and every time a new fan walked in and looked up, the first thing they saw was the Lakers' seventeen championship flags staring back at them like a pop quiz on suffering.

Let us say you are a Clippers season ticket holder. You drive to the arena, park, walk inside, look up at the ceiling, count seventeen Lakers championship banners, find your seat, and then cheer for the Clippers for three hours before driving home past Lakers billboards on the freeway. You do this forty-one times a year. You have done this for twenty years. You are either the most resilient sports fan alive or you have simply stopped looking at ceilings. Either way, you deserve recognition.

18. The Wildest Trades in Clippers History

The Los Angeles Clippers have been involved in some truly spectacular roster decisions over the years, and spectacular is doing some heavy lifting in that sentence. In the legendary 1984 draft, they picked Lancaster Gordon at number eight while future Hall of Famer John Stockton sat on the board for eight more picks. Gordon averaged under six points a game. Stockton became the NBA's all-time leader in assists and steals. That is the kind of miss that makes you want to sit quietly in a dark room.

They traded Elton Brand, one of their best players of the 2000s, in a salary dispute that led to Brand leaving as a free agent for the Philadelphia 76ers in 2008. The Clippers also famously almost acquired Kevin Durant in a 2019 deal that would have made them arguably the most stacked team in the Western Conference. Durant chose a different destination. The Clippers watched it happen from a very nice building they did not yet own.

On the positive side, the trade that brought Chris Paul to LA in 2011 was one of the most transformative roster moves in franchise history, and the decision to bring in Kawhi Leonard in 2019 showed that the organization had learned how to compete for top tier free agents.

The Clippers have gone from being the team other players avoided to a genuine destination, which required a complete rebuild of reputation, facilities, ownership, and culture. They managed all four. It just took a while. Forty years, give or take.

19. Clippers Nation: The Fans Who Showed Up Anyway

There is a specific type of person who chooses to become a Clippers fan in Los Angeles, a city where the Lakers exist and have seventeen championship banners and a century of highlight footage. That person is not making the easy choice. That person is making a statement, possibly about themselves, possibly about society, definitely about their willingness to endure things that are genuinely difficult.

Clippers fans during the losing years were a small, loud, deeply committed group who attended games in a building half-filled with people who were primarily there to watch the opposing team. They booed when the team deserved it, which was often. They cheered when something good happened, which was less often. They kept coming back, which was the most impressive part of all. Season ticket holders from the dark years would later be rewarded with seats to playoff games,

All-Star appearances, and eventually a brand-new arena, which is either the universe paying its debts or just good timing depending on your philosophical leanings.

The fanbase exploded during the Lob City era, which brought in a wave of new supporters who had never suffered through the Sterling years and arrived just in time for the highlights. The long-timers welcomed them, mostly. Every fanbase needs both the lifers who remember the pain and the newcomers who just want to enjoy the good stuff. The Clippers have both now, which means the arguments in the stands are at least interesting even when the score is not.

20. The Sterling Sale: The Day the Clippers Stopped Being a Punchline

The moment the sale closed and Steve Ballmer officially became the owner of the Los Angeles Clippers, something changed inside the league that no press release could fully capture. It was not just the money. Money had always existed in the NBA. It was the signal. A person who could have bought almost any franchise in professional sports, in any city, in any league, looked at the options available and chose the Clippers. That had simply never happened before, and the rest of the league noticed immediately.

Players around the NBA started talking about Los Angeles differently. Not Lakers-LA, the city they had always dreamed about. Clippers-LA, the team they had always politely declined to consider. Agents started returning calls from the Clippers front office a little faster. Veterans started listing the Clippers among their preferred destinations in free agency conversations. The locker room culture, which had spent decades reflecting the instability at the top, began to stabilize in ways that showed up in recruiting, retention, and the general sense that this was now a real organization run by people who intended to win rather than just exist.

The fans felt it too. Season ticket renewals went up. Merchandise actually sold. People started wearing Clippers gear in Los Angeles without immediately being asked if they meant the Lakers. None of that sounds dramatic on paper. All of it was enormous in practice. The Sterling era had made the Clippers a franchise people pitied. The sale made them a franchise people watched. There is a long distance between those two things, and the Clippers crossed it in a single afternoon in 2014.

21. The Intuit Dome: A Building They Actually Own

In August 2024, the Los Angeles Clippers opened the Intuit Dome in Inglewood, California, and it was genuinely a big deal. Not just because it was new. Not just because it cost approximately two billion dollars to build, which means Ballmer essentially spent four billion dollars total just to have a proper basketball setup, which is the kind of commitment to the sport that deserves its own trophy. It was a big deal because it was theirs.

For the first time in the franchise's fifty-plus year history, the Clippers had a home that was built for them, designed around them, and not also used for concerts featuring the banner of somebody else's seventeen championships directly above center court. The Intuit Dome seats roughly eighteen thousand fans, sits in Inglewood near the stadium where the NFL's Rams and Chargers play, and was designed from the ground up with the fan experience as the stated priority, which is either a genuine organizational philosophy or very good marketing. Based on early reviews, it seems to be both.

Ballmer has called the arena the best sports venue in the world, which is the kind of statement that requires confidence bordering on audacity, but nobody who has watched him sprint down the sideline celebrating a regular season basket in November is surprised he said it. The man does not do understatement. The Intuit Dome is his statement. It landed loudly.

22. The Halo Board and the Features That Made Everyone's Jaw Drop

The Intuit Dome's most talked-about feature is the Halo Board, a massive 360-degree display screen that wraps around the entire upper bowl of the arena like someone put a jumbo TV on a ring and decided that more was more. It is seven hundred and sixty-five feet long. It shows stats, replays, graphics, and fan content all the way around the building simultaneously, which means there is genuinely not a single bad seat in the arena when it comes to seeing what is happening on screen.

The arena also features a section called the Wall, a fan zone behind one of the baskets that is standing room only, designed to create maximum noise and energy in the building. It is modeled loosely on the standing sections in European soccer stadiums, where the loudest fans cluster together and spend entire games making as much noise as physically possible. The Wall is painted entirely in Clippers colors, the fans who stand there are encouraged to be as loud as they want, and opposing players have already mentioned it in interviews, which is exactly the point.

Imagine you are a visiting player. You are trying to shoot a free throw in the fourth quarter of a close game. Behind the basket, a wall of Clippers fans is making a sound that registers on equipment usually reserved for measuring earthquakes. Above you, a screen seven hundred and sixty-five feet long is showing your statistics in real time. Steve Ballmer is in the front row. Chuck the Condor is somewhere to your left. You bounce the ball three times and try to remember how free throws work. Good luck.

23. The Path Back to Contention: Building Without a Blueprint

After Kawhi Leonard's knee issues limited his availability through the early 2020s, the Clippers faced a genuinely difficult question that most franchises spend years trying to avoid: what do you do when your best player cannot stay healthy, your window seems to be closing, and you have committed significant financial resources to a team built around one person's ability to be on the floor? The answer the Clippers landed on was essentially to keep going and trust the process, which is easier to do when you have a new arena, a supportive billionaire owner, and a general manager willing to make aggressive moves.

James Harden arrived via trade in 2023 and brought with him a scoring ability and a step-back jumper that opponents have been trying to guard since approximately 2012 without notable success. The Clippers added depth, developed younger pieces, and maintained their position as a team capable of competing in the Western Conference on any given night even without their full roster available.

The rebuild in progress is quieter than the Lob City era and less dramatic than the Kawhi arrival, but it is real.

The organization has decided that patient construction beats desperate short-term gambles, which is a lesson that took the better part of five decades to fully learn and is now being applied with considerably better resources than were previously available. Progress is not always loud. Sometimes it looks like a team quietly getting better while everyone else is watching someone flashier down the road.

24. Clippers vs. Lakers: The Rivalry That Only One Side Admits Is a Rivalry

The Lakers and the Clippers have played in the same city since 1984. They shared the same arenas for forty years. They compete for the same free agents, the same headlines, and theoretically the same fans, though very few people in Los Angeles root for both teams and those who do are either very diplomatic or just enjoy complicated family dinners.

The traditional dynamic has been lopsided in a direction that does not favor the Clippers. The Lakers have seventeen championships. The Clippers have zero. The Lakers have retired the numbers of legends who changed the sport. The Clippers have the Intuit Dome and a mascot named after a nearly extinct bird. For most of their shared history, the Clippers were not the Lakers' rival. They were the Lakers' footnote, the other team in town that occasionally made the sports page when nothing more interesting was happening.

That dynamic has shifted meaningfully in the modern era. The Clippers have become genuine playoff contenders, drawn genuine superstar talent, and built a genuine home that no longer requires them to play under someone else's banners. Lakers fans still have the championship math on their side, which is a reasonable point. Clippers fans have the future on their side, which is an equally reasonable point. The rivalry is more balanced than it has ever been, which might be the single most surprising sentence in this entire book.

25. The Future Is Now: What Comes Next for Clippers Nation

The Los Angeles Clippers enter this chapter of their history with something they have almost never had before: genuine reasons for optimism that are based on actual evidence rather than hope alone. They have a state-of-the-art arena. They have an owner who behaves like he personally invented the concept of enthusiasm. They have a roster with proven talent and a front office that has demonstrated the ability to attract and retain players who have other options.

The question is no longer whether the Clippers belong in the conversation. They clearly do. The question is whether this particular version of the roster, in this particular window, with this particular collection of parts, can get to the NBA Finals and win the championship that has been the missing piece for the entire franchise's existence. Every team in the league asks that question every season. Most of them do not have a reasonable answer. The Clippers, for maybe the first time in their history, do.

The condor nearly went extinct and came back. The franchise went from Buffalo to San Diego to a rented corner of someone else's city to a two-billion-dollar building they built themselves. The fanbase went from a few hundred stubborn believers to a legitimate sold-out arena crowd that shakes the walls in a purpose-built section designed specifically for maximum noise. None of it happened quickly. None of it was easy. All of it was worth it. Clippers Nation has been waiting a long time for this. The Intuit Dome is open. The Halo Board is lit. Chuck the Condor is fully caffeinated and ready to go. The only thing left is the banner.

Bonus Trivia Quiz!

You think you are a true LA Clippers fan? Try this bonus quiz!

1. What city did the Clippers play in before they were called the Clippers?

A) San Diego
B) Seattle
C) Buffalo
D) Detroit

2. What was the original name of the franchise when it was founded in 1970?

A) The Buffalo Blizzard
B) The Buffalo Braves
C) The Buffalo Bulls
D) The Buffalo Blazers

3. Why did the NBA fine Donald Sterling six million dollars in 1984?

A) He refused to pay player salaries on time
B) He moved the team to Los Angeles without the league's permission
C) He missed the NBA owners' annual meeting three years in a row
D) He wore the wrong outfit to a press conference

4. Bob McAdoo won three consecutive NBA scoring titles. Which years were they?

A) 1971, 1972, 1973
B) 1974, 1975, 1976
C) 1977, 1978, 1979
D) 1980, 1981, 1982

5. What did Lloyd Free legally change his name to?

A) Free B. World
B) B. World Free
C) World B. Free
D) Freedom B. Lloyd

6. Danny Manning was selected first overall in the 1988 NBA Draft out of which college?

A) Duke

B) Kentucky

C) Kansas

D) North Carolina

7. What injury derailed Danny Manning's first NBA season with the Clippers?

A) Broken wrist

B) Torn Achilles

C) Stress fracture in his foot

D) Torn ACL

8. Which player combination was the heart of the "Lob City" era?

A) Kawhi Leonard and Paul George

B) Chris Paul, Blake Griffin, and DeAndre Jordan

C) Danny Manning and Ron Harper

D) James Harden and Reggie Jackson

9. Blake Griffin won the 2011 NBA Slam Dunk Contest by jumping over what?

A) A motorcycle

B) A teammate sitting in a chair

C) A Kia car

D) A table stacked with equipment

10. How much did Steve Ballmer pay to buy the Clippers in 2014?

A) Five hundred million dollars

B) One billion dollars

C) One and a half billion dollars

D) Two billion dollars

11. What is the name of the Clippers' official mascot?

A) Claw the Condor

B) Chuck the Condor

C) Clipper the Condor

D) Carlos the Condor

12. The Clippers reached the Western Conference Finals for the first time in franchise history in which year?

A) 2015

B) 2019

C) 2021

D) 2023

13. The Clippers' new arena in Inglewood features a massive 360-degree display called what?

A) The Ring
B) The Halo Board
C) The Crown
D) The Circle

14. How many years did the Clippers share an arena with the Lakers before getting their own building?

A) Twenty years
B) Thirty years
C) Forty years
D) Fifty years

15. Which former Microsoft CEO bought the Clippers in 2014?

A) Bill Gates
B) Paul Allen
C) Satya Nadella
D) Steve Ballmer

Super Fan Secret Challenge

Only a true LA Clippers fan will know this.

(No Answer Provided)

The Clippers spent forty years playing in arenas owned by other organizations before finally opening their own building in 2024. Name the three different arenas the Clippers called home during their time in Los Angeles before the Intuit Dome opened.

Answer Key

1. C) Buffalo

2. B) The Buffalo Braves

3. B) He moved the team to Los Angeles without the league's permission

4. B) 1974, 1975, 1976

5. C) World B. Free

6. C) Kansas

7. D) Torn ACL

8. B) Chris Paul, Blake Griffin, and DeAndre Jordan

9. C) A Kia car

10. D) Two billion dollars

11. B) Chuck the Condor

12. C) 2021

13. B) The Halo Board

14. C) Forty years

15. D) Steve Ballmer

NBA PLAYOFF BRACKET

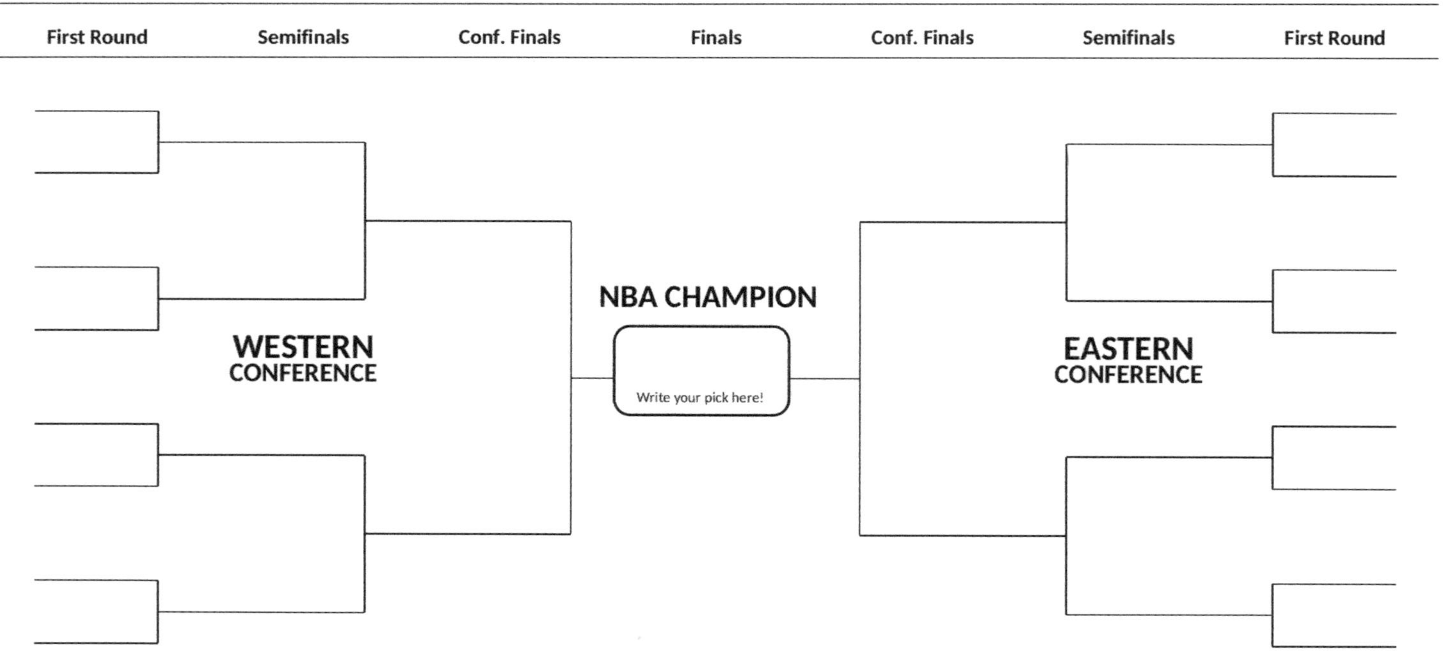

* Fill in your picks and try not to argue with your friends about it!

Part of the Fun Fan Facts: The Unofficial Sports Guide Series

Be the Boss of the Playoffs

You've broken down the matchups. You know which superstar takes over in the fourth quarter. You've seen the bench units that quietly decide series. You've watched the adjustments coaches make when their backs are against the wall.

Now it's time to stop watching and start deciding.

On this page, you are not just a fan. You are the Head Coach drawing up the last play with three seconds left on the clock. You are the GM who built this roster. You are the analyst who saw it all coming.

This is not just filling out a bracket.

This is building your championship run.

Sixteen teams enter the NBA Playoffs. The path is brutal. Best of seven. No shortcuts. No hiding. Every round gets louder, harder, and more personal.

This bracket is your Playoff Control Room.

The Game Plan

1. Survive Round One: Start with the opening round. Which matchup is going seven games? Who has the closer? Who folds under pressure? Make the calls.

2. Feel the Momentum: As you move into the Conference Semifinals and Conference Finals, things change. Role players become heroes. Stars feel the weight. Trust your reads.

3. Own the Finals: Trace your picks all the way to the NBA Finals. When the confetti falls and the trophy is raised, you'll find out who earned it.

House Rules: Circle your boldest upset. That is your official "I knew it" moment.

Choose Your Weapon: Pencil if you want flexibility. Pen if you trust your instincts. Sharpie if you believe in chaos.

Because once the playoffs tip off, there is no rewinding Game 7.

Make your picks. Trust your basketball brain. And let the playoff drama begin.

Fun Facts Wrap-Up

You made it through! You're officially a true superfan! Now it's time to put your knowledge to the test. Share these facts with friends and see who really knows their team best.

Love the series?

Your reviews help other fans discover Fun Fan Facts. If you enjoyed this book, we'd really appreciate you sharing your thoughts and leaving a review.

Want more Fun Fan Facts?

Scan the QR code below to visit our site and explore bonus trivia, challenges, and special extras - including new teams, future series, and collectible fun as they're released.

Collect All the Fun Fan Facts Series!

Check off every book you read. See the full set on Amazon. Search "Fun Fan Facts Jake Liam."

World Cup 2026 Edition

☐ Algeria	☐ Scotland	☐ Morocco
☐ France	☐ Brazil	☐ Switzerland
☐ Paraguay	☐ Ivory Coast	☐ Curaçao
☐ Argentina	☐ Senegal	☐ Netherlands
☐ Germany	☐ Canada	☐ Tunisia
☐ Portugal	☐ Japan	☐ Ecuador
☐ Australia	☐ South Africa	☐ New Zealand
☐ Ghana	☐ Cape Verde	☐ United States
☐ Qatar	☐ Jordan	☐ Egypt
☐ Austria	☐ South Korea	☐ Norway
☐ Haiti	☐ Colombia	☐ Uruguay
☐ Saudi Arabia	☐ Mexico	☐ England
☐ Belgium	☐ Spain	☐ Panama
☐ Iran	☐ Croatia	☐ Uzbekistan

World Cup 2026 Group Edition

☐ Group A	☐ Group F	☐ Group K
☐ Group E	☐ Group J	☐ Group D
☐ Group I	☐ Group C	☐ Group H
☐ Group B	☐ Group G	☐ Group L

English Football Edition

☐ Arsenal F.C.

☐ Aston Villa F.C.

☐ Chelsea F.C.

☐ Everton F.C.

☐ Fulham F.C.

☐ Liverpool F.C.

☐ Manchester City

☐ Manchester United

☐ Newcastle United F.C.

☐ Tottenham Hotspur

☐ West Ham United

☐ Wrexham A.F.C.

NBA Edition

☐ Atlanta Hawks

☐ Boston Celtics

☐ Brooklyn Nets

☐ Charlotte Hornets

☐ Chicago Bulls

☐ Cleveland Cavaliers

☐ Dallas Mavericks

☐ Denver Nuggets

☐ Detroit Pistons

☐ Golden State Warriors

☐ Houston Rockets

☐ Indiana Pacers

☐ LA Clippers

☐ Los Angeles Lakers

☐ Memphis Grizzlies

☐ Miami Heat

☐ Milwaukee Bucks

☐ Minnesota Timberwolves

☐ New Orleans Pelicans

☐ New York Knicks

☐ Oklahoma City Thunder

☐ Orlando Magic

☐ Philadelphia 76ers

☐ Phoenix Suns

☐ Portland Trail Blazers

☐ Sacramento Kings

☐ San Antonio Spurs

☐ Toronto Raptors

☐ Utah Jazz

☐ Washington Wizards

About the Author

Jake is a 13-year-old sports fan who loves football, American football, and basketball. He plays soccer as a goalie and dreams of one day playing for West Ham United and helping teach kids to love the game. His passion for sports runs in the family - his dad was a professional baseball player, and his stepdad sparked his love for West Ham. Through the Fun Fan Facts series, he shares the fun and excitement of sports with fans everywhere.